This Book Belongs To:
_____

Disney's MICKEY MOUSE Stories

With an introduction by *Mickey Mouse*

Hello, Everybody!

I love wonderful stories more than just about anything in the whole, wide world. And stories about princes, dragons, giants, and good deeds are my all-time favorite kind—especially when I pretend I'm the hero and save Minnie from disaster!

Read one of my magical tales with your mom or dad, with your sister, brother, or grandma, with your baby-sitter or your best friend—heck, with just about anybody you love—right before bedtime or any time you feel like a good story.

Love,
Mickey Mouse

Contents

Sir Mickey Hits the Spot

Once upon a time, there was a happy little kingdom with one big problem. A fire-breathing dragon lived in a nearby cave. Every few weeks the dragon burned down a different village in the land. The king sent messengers out with this decree: "To the knight who rids the land of the terrible dragon, the king will give a room filled with gold, a kingdom of his own, or the hand of Princess Minnie."

Brave Sir Donald, Sir Goofy, and Sir Mickey rode out
of the castle, each dreaming of the prize he hoped to win.
Sir Mickey raised his sword and cried, "Let's go save
the kingdom!"

Sir Donald shouted, "Come on out, you fire-breathing kingdom wrecker!"

The dragon answered with a roar and a burst of flame aimed right at the plucky knight.

"Yeow!" cried Sir Donald.

Sir Goofy said, "Hiya, dragon! Why did the little dragon cross the playground?"

The dragon didn't know.

"To get to the other slide!" Sir Goofy said. Then he read the riddle again . . . and again . . . and again . . .

. . . and again. Sir Goofy hoped to bore the dragon to death. But this big dragon had a tiny memory. He liked to hear the same riddle over and over because he could never remember the answer.

"Golly, now it's up to me to save the kingdom," Sir Mickey
gulped. Bravely, he blew a handful of pepper into the dragon's
face. As the dragon opened his mouth to sneeze . . .

. . . Sir Mickey used his shield to prop it open. Then he tossed water down the dragon's throat.

The dragon's sneeze was just smoke—the fire was out. "Thanks! That hit the spot!" said the dragon.

"I couldn't remember how to put out the fire," the dragon said sadly. "When I tried to ask for help—well, you know what happened."

Sir Mickey had another good idea. "This sign will help you remember," he said.

Sir Mickey received a hero's welcome. There were parades and parties and the biggest, most wonderful wedding ever. The whole kingdom was invited . . . including the dragon.

Hansel Mickey and Gretel Minnie

Once upon a time, there lived a poor servant named Mickey. He worked for the blacksmith. The work was hard and the blacksmith was mean, but Mickey stayed because next door lived Minnie, the poor servant of the baker, who was as angry and mean as the blacksmith.

At one time, the blacksmith and baker had been wealthy and kind. But long ago a witch had stolen their hearts, along with their fortunes.

Mickey loved Minnie more than anything. Her tears hurt him more than all the blacksmith's beatings.

"Minnie," he called softly. "Tonight the moon will be full. Let's run away."

Mickey and Minnie walked through the forest for hours and hours. Tired and hungry, they were about to stop, when Minnie saw something in the distance.

"Look, Mickey," she cried. "A cottage!"

"A delicious cottage" said Mickey, tasting a piece of
gingerbread windowsill.

The gingerbread cottage door opened. "Come in, come in.
You must be tired and hungry," said an old woman.

It was the most wonderful meal the two poor servants ever tasted—vegetables and meats, fruits and breads, cakes and pies, and fresh milk to drink. The big meal made them very, very sleepy.

Mickey awoke in a cage.

"When I've fattened you up, you will make a tasty servant's pie," cackled the old woman. Then she yelled, "Girl, knead the bread! Mix the batter! Faster! Smoother!"

"Light the oven!" the old woman demanded next.

Minnie said, "The baker always lit the oven herself."

The old woman sneered. "Ah, yes, the baker. Does she miss her fortune and her heart very much?"

"You're the witch who stole all the kindness from the blacksmith and the baker," cried Mickey.

Then Minnie pushed the witch right into the oven. With one hand she slammed the oven door shut, and with the other she set Mickey free.

Mickey and Minnie found the stolen hearts and fortunes in the witch's attic. So with the hearts back in the right place and wealth enough for all, the baker, the blacksmith, and Mickey and Minnie lived happily ever after.

Mickey and the Beanstalk

Once upon a time, a golden harp lived in a beautiful castle. The harp's magic song cast a spell of peace and plenty over the land. Everyone was happy in the land called Happy Valley.

One day the magic harp disappeared. Lush fields turned to dust. Rivers ran dry. Mickey, Donald, and Goofy were down to their last slice of bread and their last three beans.

Sadly, Mickey sold their cow, Bossy. He bought . . .

"Beans?" Donald sputtered. "You sold Bossy for a bunch of beans?" Donald threw them down before Mickey could say, "Wait. They're magic beans!"

As the farmers slept, the magic beans grew. . . and grew. . .
and grew. The beanstalk lifted the house up, up, up into the sky.
"Gawrsh!" cried Goofy, "There's a castle in the clouds."

In the castle, Mickey, Donald, and Goofy discovered giant-sized food. They ate and ate and ate.

Then they heard a soft voice say, "Who's there?" It was the harp. She was locked inside a box.

"Beware of the wicked giant who kidnapped me," she warned them.

"Fee-fi-fo-fum, I smell turkey!" the giant's voice boomed. "Yum, yum, yum! I smell bread! I smell pies! I smell . . .?

. . . spies!" The giant grabbed Mickey, Donald, and Goofy and opened the wooden box. He put them in and took the magic harp out.

But Mickey slipped out before the giant could lock the box.

"Sing," demanded the giant.

The harp sang so sweetly that the giant was soon asleep.

Mickey unlocked the box and his friends jumped out. The farmers picked up the harp and raced out of the castle.

"Hurry, Mickey, hurry!" cried the harp. Mickey leaped to the ground just as Donald and Goofy sawed through the beanstalk.

CRASH! The beanstalk and the giant came tumbling down.

With the magic harp back in her castle, crops grew, rivers ran, and laughter filled the air.

But happiest of all were the three brave farmers. They had saved Happy Valley from the wicked giant.

Brave Little Tailor

Once upon a time, there was a tailor named Mickey Mouse. He lived in a kingdom ruled by a good king and the beautiful Princess Minnie. All was well in the land until a terrible giant appeared.

The king offered a rich reward to get rid of the giant.

"Have you ever killed a giant?" the butcher asked the baker. Before the baker could answer, Mickey proclaimed, "I killed seven with one blow!"

Now, Mickey was talking about flies, not giants. But he was called before the royal court. And before he could explain he had killed seven flies, not giants, Mickey was appointed Royal High Giant Slayer.

Before he could say "giant slayer" three times fast, Mickey was sent to work. Out into the country he went in search of the giant.

"Yikes!" cried Mickey, leaping into a cart of pumpkins.

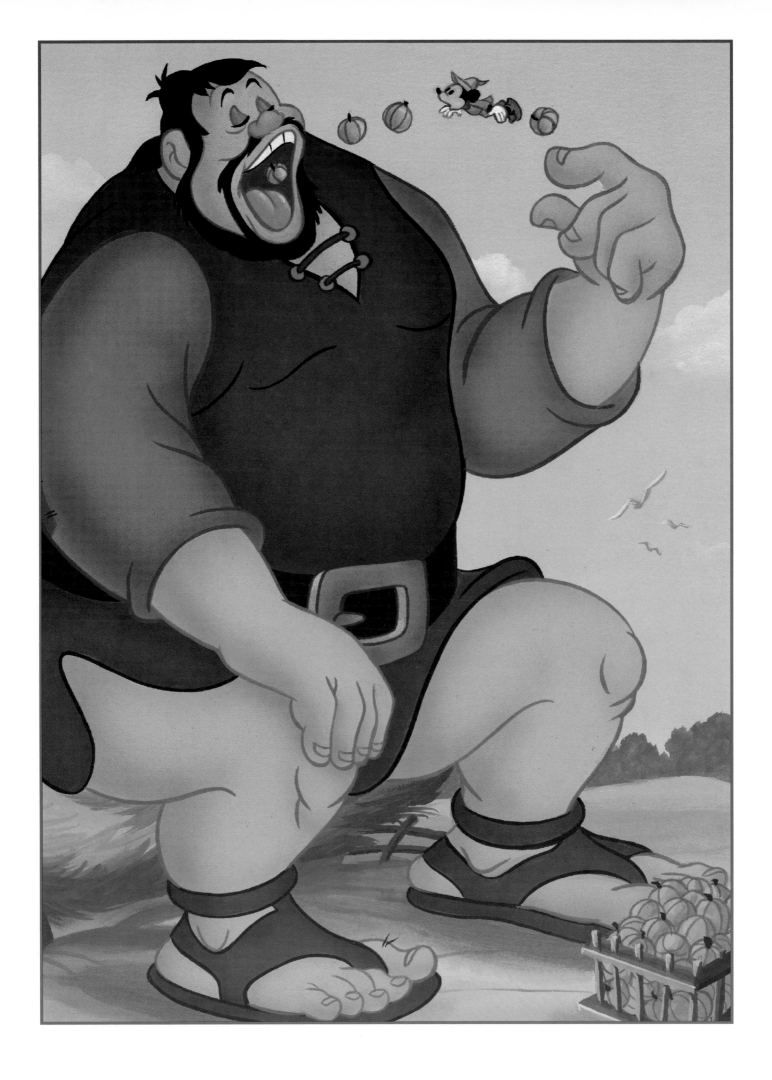

"Food!" exclaimed the giant, reaching into the pile of pumpkins.

To the giant, pumpkins were no bigger than grapes. He popped them into his mouth. And he popped Mickey in, too!

To wash down the pumpkin snack, the giant pulled a well right out of the ground. As the giant drank, Mickey grabbed the bucket from the well.

Mickey leaped from the bucket onto the giant's arm.
Then the brave little tailor slipped under the giant's shirt
and crawled up into his sleeve.

A giant hand chased Mickey into the sleeve. Mickey used his tailor's scissors to cut his way out. Then, when the giant's hand followed him out of the sleeve, he sewed up the hole. The giant's hand was caught in his own sleeve!

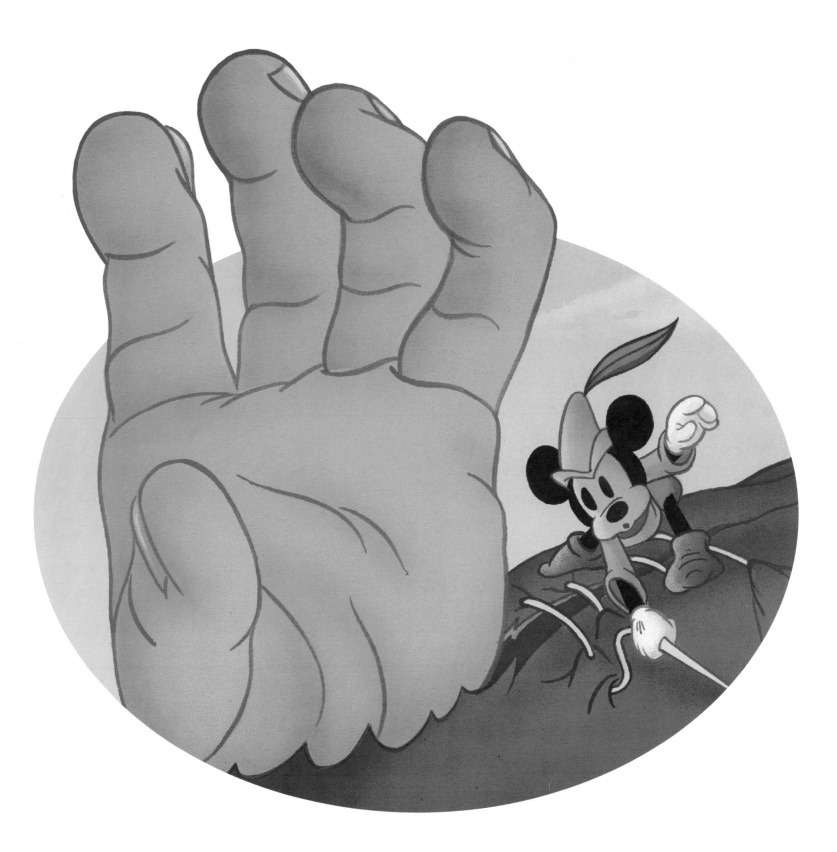

Round and round the giant Mickey swung, tying him up
with thread. When the giant tried to get away, he stumbled
and fell. The terrible giant hit his head and passed out. Soon
he was snoring soundly.

The brave little tailor had neatly sewed up the kingdom's giant problem. His reward was one million golden pazoozahs and the love of Princess Minnie.

Naturally Mickey and the princess lived happily ever after.

The Prince and the Pauper

Once upon a time, Mickey and his friends were poor, humble subjects of a good king. Even when Mickey was cold and hungry, he never lost hope that one day his luck would change.

"Pluto, come here!" called Mickey.

But Pluto was chasing a royal coach—right into the palace! Mickey knocked on the gate.

The gatekeeper bowed and said, "Y-Y-Your Majesty! Come in, Sire."

Captain Pete, the wicked captain of the guards, grabbed
Mickey, and Pluto began to bark.

"I just want my dog," Mickey said. The ruckus brought
the prince to the window.

"Captain, the king is ill and needs quiet. What's this racket?" cried the prince.

Pete said, "Local riffraff, Sire."

"Every subject deserves respect. Bring him to me!" commanded the prince.

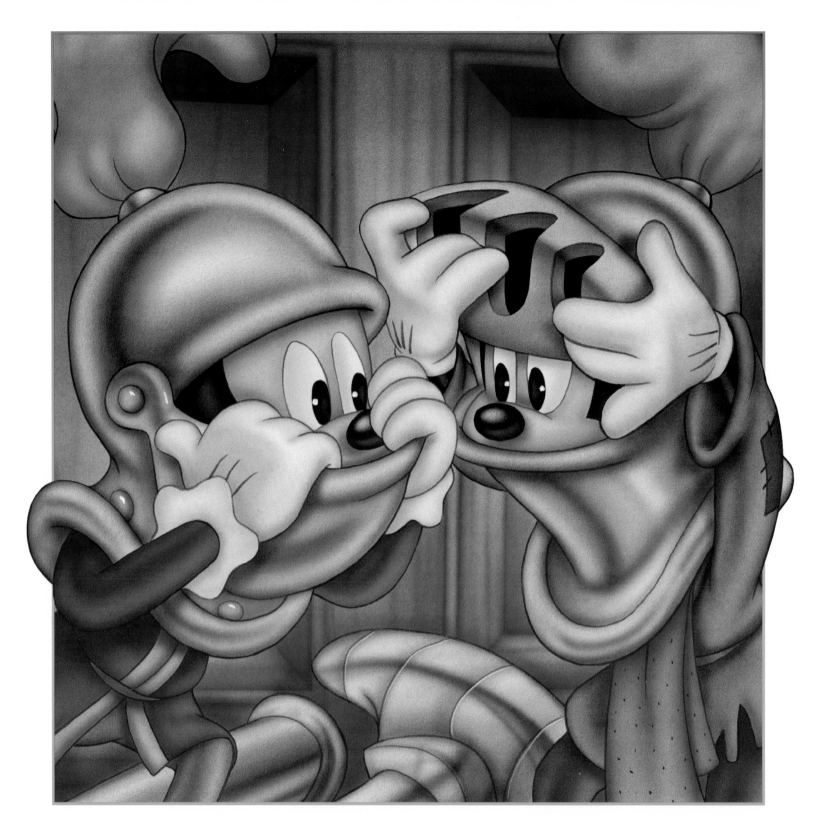

"You look like me!" they both exclaimed.

This gave the prince an idea. "Let's trade places." Even dressed in rags, the prince was sure his royal ring would identify him to his people.

So, while the prince went off to town, Mickey went to the prince's lessons.

Donald, the prince's valet, came in with lunch. But before Mickey could eat it, Donald had "tasted" all the food.

The prince learned that life outside the palace was not all fun and games. "Stealing in the king's name?" he cried. "Unhand that hen, in the name of the prince!"

The guard just laughed.

Back in the palace, Captain Pete realized that Mickey was not the prince. So he went to Goofy's house and arrested the real prince. Then he put the prince in the dungeon with Donald.

Goofy to the rescue! In disguise, he entered the dungeon.
Then he tripped the guard and knocked him out. The freed
prince, with Donald, Goofy, and Pluto, fought and disarmed
the evil Pete.

At last the real prince was crowned king.

"Long live the king!" everyone shouted. The new king, with the help of his loyal friends, Mickey, Pluto, Goofy, and Donald, ruled as justly and wisely as his father had done.

The Sorcerer's Apprentice

Once upon a time, Mickey was apprenticed to a mighty sorcerer. Mickey swept the floors, filled the cauldron with water, dusted the book of spells, and dreamed of being a powerful sorcerer himself.

After a long night of spectacular spells and potent potions, the weary sorcerer said, "Tidy the study and fill the cauldron, Mickey. But do not touch the magic hat. Its power is beyond your control."

Mickey yawned. The cauldron was
very big and the well was very deep.
The apprentice sighed as he began
his chores.

On top of the book of spells,
the sorcerer's magic hat
glowed invitingly.

"One itty bitty spell won't hurt," said Mickey softly, placing the magic hat on his head. "It fits!" he cried.

Suddenly, Mickey's mind filled with magnificent magic and sweet sorcery.

"I am Sorcerer Mickey," he announced. Then with an "abracadabra," a flick of the wrist, and some fancy finger-wiggle-waggling, the broom sprang to life!

On legs made of straw, the broom carried buckets from the well to fill the cauldron. Back and forth it went—well to cauldron, well to cauldron.

Now, a magic broom never tires, never wavers . . .

. . . but Sorcerer Mickey did. Sitting in the sorcerer's comfy chair, he fell asleep. While he dozed, the broom continued to carry buckets of water from the well, filling the cauldron again and again.

Water sloshing over the stone floor woke Mickey up.

"Oh, no! Stop, broom! Stop!" cried Mickey. The broom wouldn't listen. Mickey grabbed an axe and cut the broom into little pieces. Instead of stopping one broom, Mickey created dozens of brooms—all of them carrying buckets of water to the already overflowing cauldron!

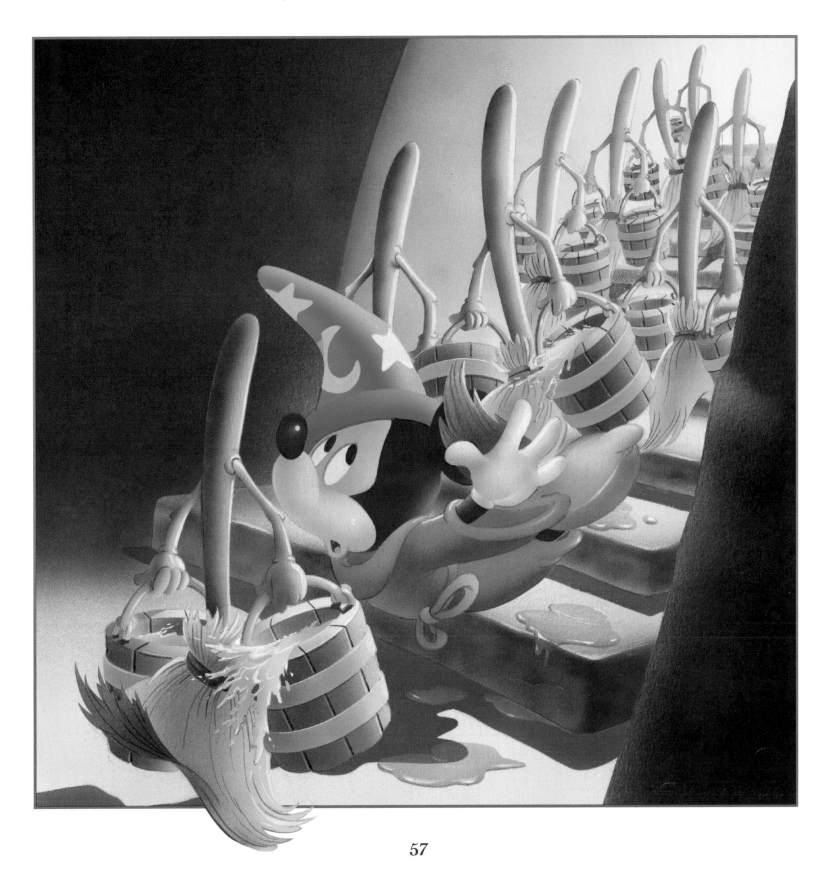

The floodwaters rose higher and higher. As Sorcerer Mickey clung to the book of spells, he wished with all his might that the sorcerer would appear.

Finally the mighty sorcerer did appear. He made the water disappear. The broom became just a broom, and Sorcerer Mickey was once again just a sorcerer's apprentice—a very sorry sorcerer's apprentice.

"Sir Mickey Hits the Spot" by Liane B. Onish; illustrated by
Peter Emslie, Carson Van Osten, and Don Williams.

"Hansel Mickey and Gretel Minnie" by Liane B. Onish; illustrated by
Peter Emslie, Carson Van Osten, and Don Williams.

"Mickey and the Beanstalk," based on the original story by
Bruce Talkington; adapted by Liane B. Onish; illustrated by Phil Wilson.

"The Brave Little Tailor," based on the original story by Bruce Talkington; adapted by
Liane B. Onish; illustrated by Peter Emslie, Carson Van Osten, and Don Williams.

"The Prince and the Pauper," based on the original story by Bruce Talkington; adapted by
Liane B. Onish; illustrated by Phil Wilson.

"The Sorcerer's Apprentice," based on the original story by Bruce Talkington; adapted by
Liane B. Onish; illustrated by Franc Mateau.

For information address Mouse Works, 114 Fifth Avenue, New York, New York 10011-5690.
First Edition.
Printed in the United States of America.
ISBN 0-7364-0030-3
10 9 8 7 6 5 4 3 2 1